YOUR BODY BATTLES A BROKEN BONE

WRITTEN BY **VICKI COBB**   PHOTOMICROGRAPHS BY **DENNIS KUNKEL**

ILLUSTRATIONS BY **ANDREW N. HARRIS**

M̲ Millbrook Press / Minneapolis

NOTE: The photomicrographs in this book were taken with a scanning electron microscope (SEM). The photos are originally in black and white. A computer program is used to add color, often to highlight interesting features. The colors used do not show the real colors of the subject. The × followed by a number indicates magnification. For example, ×250 means the object in the picture is 250 times larger than its real size.

For Jillian Davis Cobb —VC

This series is dedicated to my mom, Carmen Kunkel, for the care she gives her children and grandchildren —DK

For Jean, thank you for the experience and opportunities —ANH

With special thanks to Dr. Robert I, Cristofaro, Clinical Associate Professor of Orthopaedic Surgery, New York Medical College, Valhalla, NY, and Director of Pediatric Orthopaedic Surgery Westchester Medical Center, Valhalla, NY; Dr. Sue Ott, Associate Professor of Medicine, University of Washington; and thanks also to Mary Slamin and Gail Fell, children's librarians from the Greenburgh, New York Public Library, for assistance with the Further Reading list.

Text copyright © 2009 by Vicki Cobb
Photomicrographs © 2009 by Dennis Kunkel
Illustrations copyright © 2009 by Lerner Publishing Group, Inc.

Additional photographs in this book are reproduced with the permission of: © Edward Kinsman/Photo Researchers, Inc., pp. 14, 16; © Eye of Science/Photo Researchers, Inc., p. 27.

Millbrook Press
A division of Lerner Publishing Group, Inc.
241 First Avenue North
Minneapolis, MN 55401 U.S.A.

Website address: www.lernerbooks.com

Library of Congress Cataloging-in-Publication Data

Cobb, Vicki.
     Your body battles a broken bone / by Vicki Cobb ; with photomicrographs by Dennis Kunkel ; illustrations by Andrew N. Harris.
       p.   cm. — (Body Battles)
     Includes bibliographical references and index.
     ISBN 978-0-8225-7468-2 (lib. bdg. : alk. paper)   3991 4766 · 04/09
     1. Bones—Wounds and injuries—Juvenile literature. I. Harris, Andrew, 1977– ill. II. Title.
   RD101.C63 2009
   617.4'71044—dc22   20080028337

Manufactured in the United States of America
1 2 3 4 5 6 – DP – 14 13 12 11 10 09

A broken bone happens quickly, and it's a nasty surprise. First, you feel a sharp pain. Then you feel a deep ache that doesn't go away. Your whole body reacts to the break. You might feel cold. You might feel dizzy and even pass out.

The good news is that you will recover. Different parts of your body work as a team to put your broken bone back together—with the help of a doctor, of course. Meet the superheroes of your own body. This book tells their story.

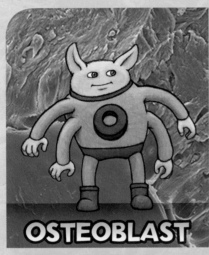
OSTEOBLAST

NEUTROPHIL

FIBROBLAST

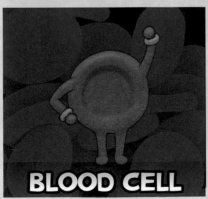
BLOOD CELL

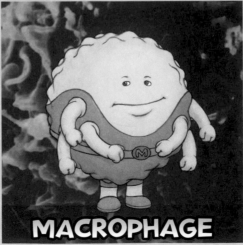
MACROPHAGE

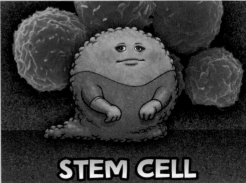
STEM CELL

Your bones support your entire body. Without them, you would be a blob. Your muscles attach to your bones so that you can move. Like the rest of your body, your bones are alive. Your whole body is made of tiny living things called cells.

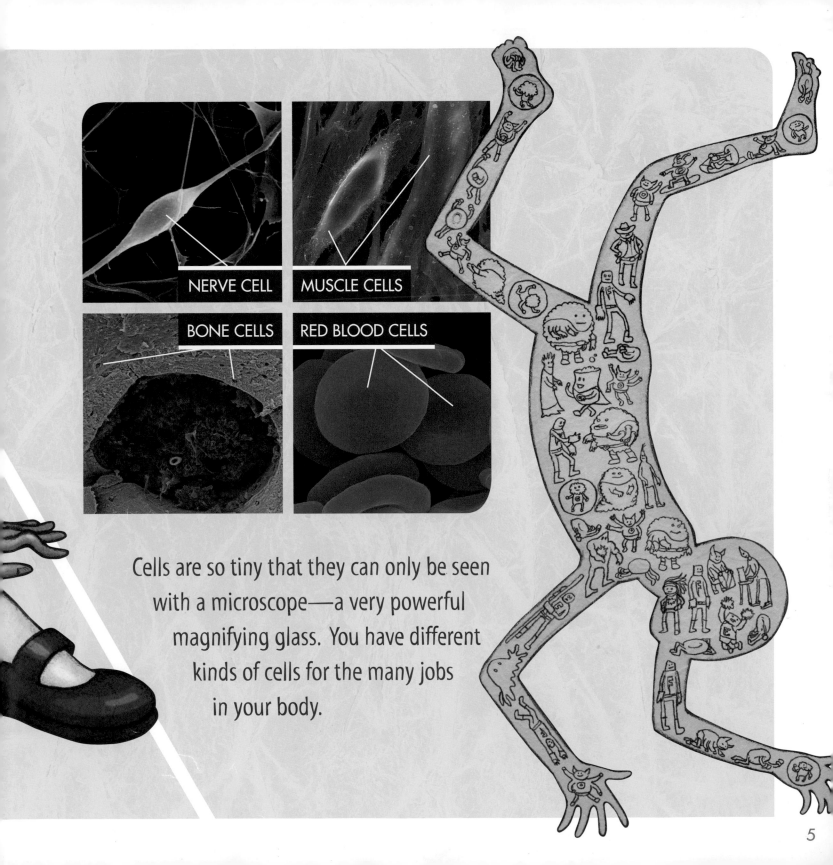

NERVE CELL

MUSCLE CELLS

BONE CELLS

RED BLOOD CELLS

Cells are so tiny that they can only be seen with a microscope—a very powerful magnifying glass. You have different kinds of cells for the many jobs in your body.

Inside your body, there are two kinds of bone. Compact bone, also known as cortical bone, is hard and very strong. It makes up the shafts of long bones. Under the microscope, we can see that compact bone is packed in layers around a tiny central hole. This hole is actually a hollow tube, or canal, that holds very small blood vessels and nerves. Blood flowing through these blood vessels brings food and oxygen to the bone cells, or osteocytes.

COMPACT BONE CROSS SECTION ×1075

BLOOD VESSELS

BONE MARROW CAVITY

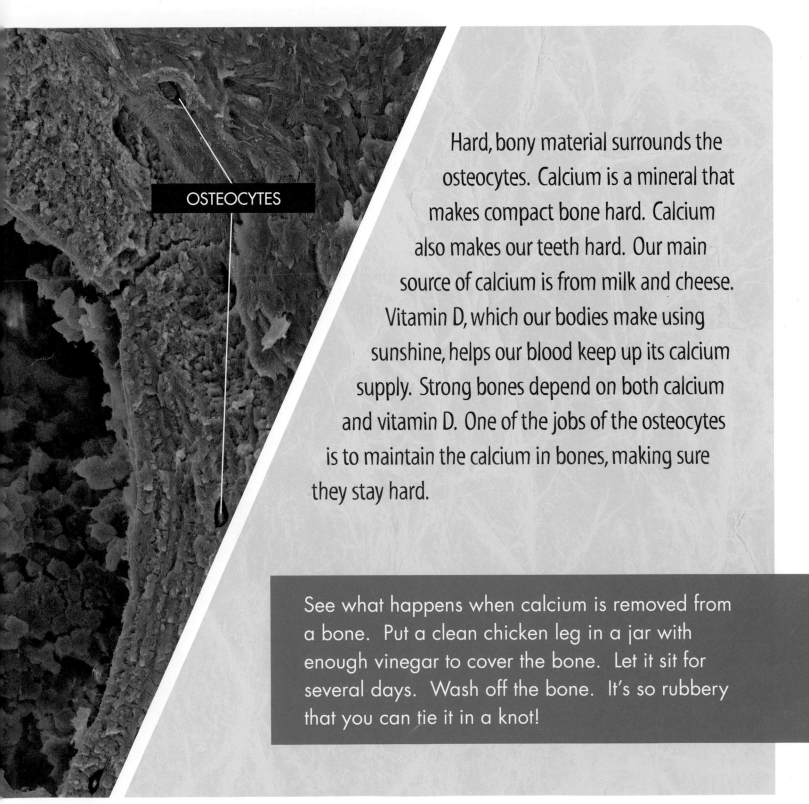

OSTEOCYTES

Hard, bony material surrounds the osteocytes. Calcium is a mineral that makes compact bone hard. Calcium also makes our teeth hard. Our main source of calcium is from milk and cheese. Vitamin D, which our bodies make using sunshine, helps our blood keep up its calcium supply. Strong bones depend on both calcium and vitamin D. One of the jobs of the osteocytes is to maintain the calcium in bones, making sure they stay hard.

See what happens when calcium is removed from a bone. Put a clean chicken leg in a jar with enough vinegar to cover the bone. Let it sit for several days. Wash off the bone. It's so rubbery that you can tie it in a knot!

×135

If you break open a chicken bone, you can see the spongy bone inside. You can also see the red bone marrow.

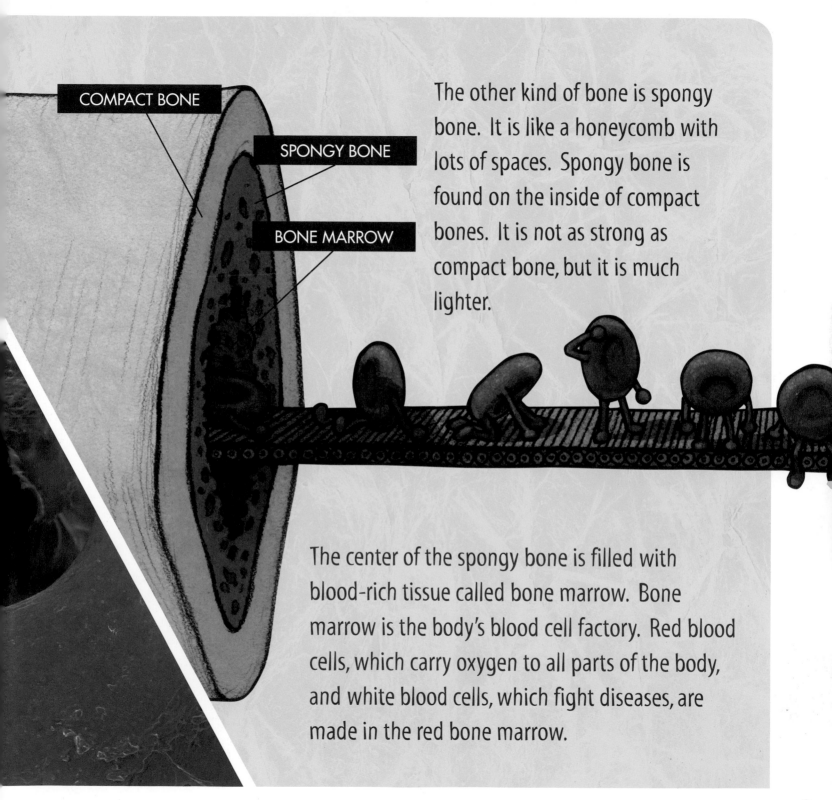

COMPACT BONE

SPONGY BONE

BONE MARROW

The other kind of bone is spongy bone. It is like a honeycomb with lots of spaces. Spongy bone is found on the inside of compact bones. It is not as strong as compact bone, but it is much lighter.

The center of the spongy bone is filled with blood-rich tissue called bone marrow. Bone marrow is the body's blood cell factory. Red blood cells, which carry oxygen to all parts of the body, and white blood cells, which fight diseases, are made in the red bone marrow.

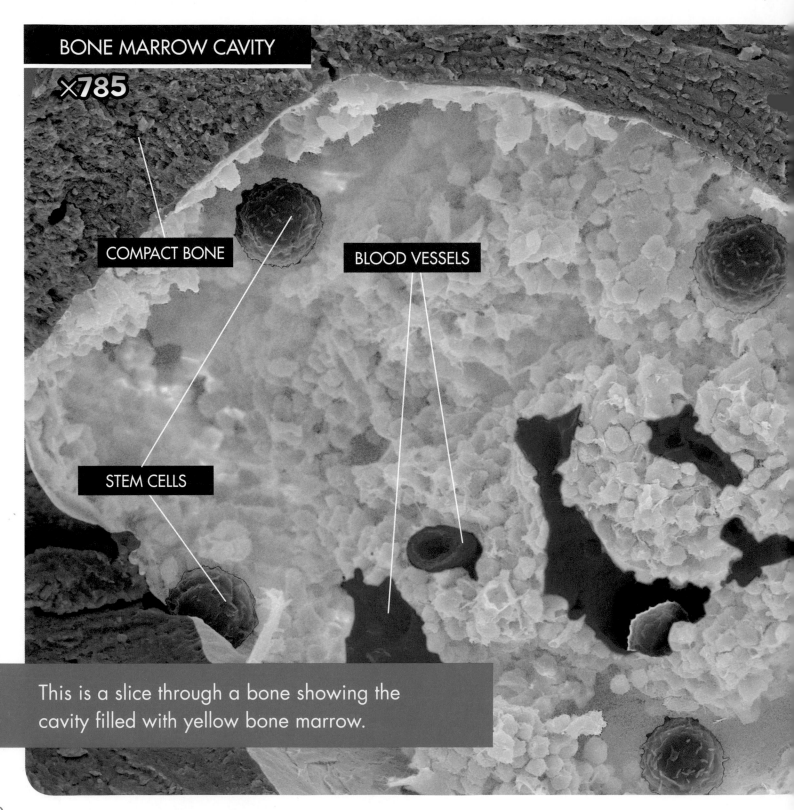

BONE MARROW CAVITY

×785

COMPACT BONE

BLOOD VESSELS

STEM CELLS

This is a slice through a bone showing the cavity filled with yellow bone marrow.

OSTEOCYTES

When you are about five years old, the marrow in the center of long bones becomes yellow instead of red. The yellow color is due to the fat stored there.

The yellow bone marrow can change back to red and make red blood cells in case a lot of blood is lost. Some white blood cells are also formed in the yellow bone marrow.

The cells in the bone marrow that make the blood cells are stem cells. All new blood cells start out as stem cells. Stem cells are amazing because they can become many other kinds of cells. You'll find out more about them later in this story.

A broken bone, like any injury, damages cells so that they start dying. The injury breaks blood vessels and destroys muscle cells in and around the bone as well. The damaged bone cells give off a chemical that is a signal to the rest of the body that help is needed.

The liquid part of blood is straw colored. Blood is red because it is full of tiny red blood cells. A drop of blood has about five million red blood cells in it. Blood also carries white blood cells. These are actually clear.

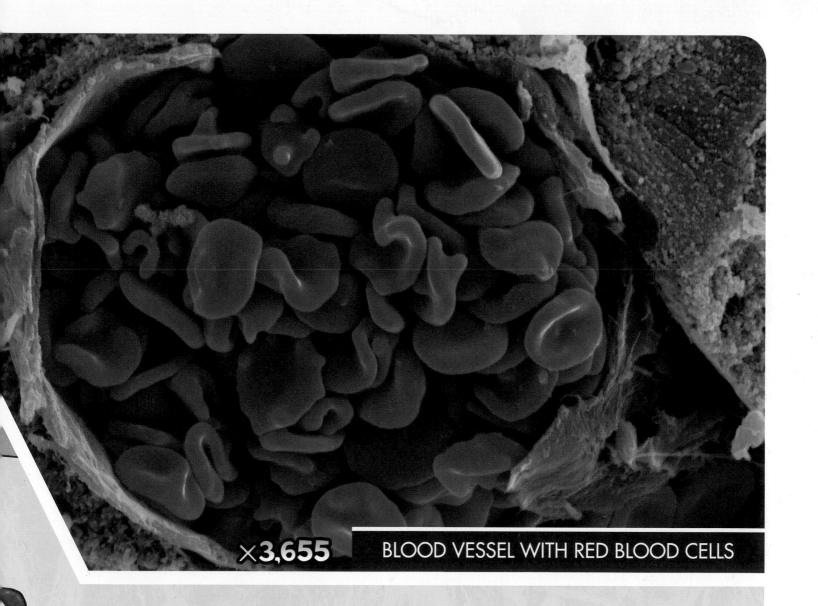

×3,655   BLOOD VESSEL WITH RED BLOOD CELLS

Blood immediately rushes to the rescue. Since a number of blood vessels are broken, some of the blood seeps into the area and causes swelling. In a few days, the blood may show through the skin as a colorful bruise.

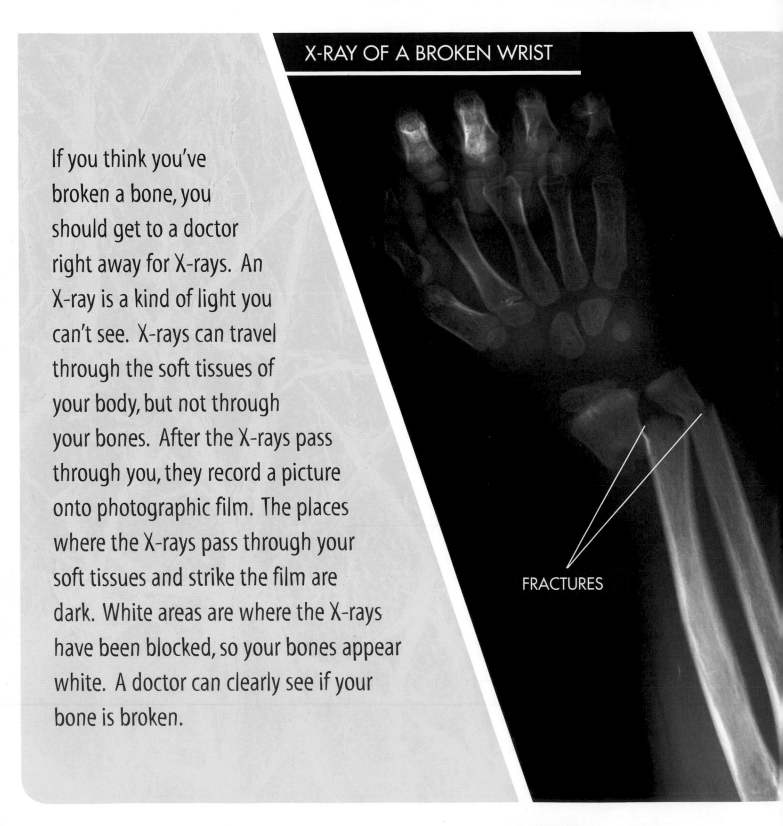

If you think you've broken a bone, you should get to a doctor right away for X-rays. An X-ray is a kind of light you can't see. X-rays can travel through the soft tissues of your body, but not through your bones. After the X-rays pass through you, they record a picture onto photographic film. The places where the X-rays pass through your soft tissues and strike the film are dark. White areas are where the X-rays have been blocked, so your bones appear white. A doctor can clearly see if your bone is broken.

FRACTURES

Most broken bones are caused by a fall. The most common bone to break is in the wrist because it's natural to stick out your hand when you feel yourself falling. Your wrist takes the force of your landing as you try to stop a fall.

The X-ray tells the doctor if the bone needs to be moved into position or if pins have to be put in to hold it in place. Don't worry. If your break needs this kind of treatment, you'll be given some medicine so you won't feel any pain.

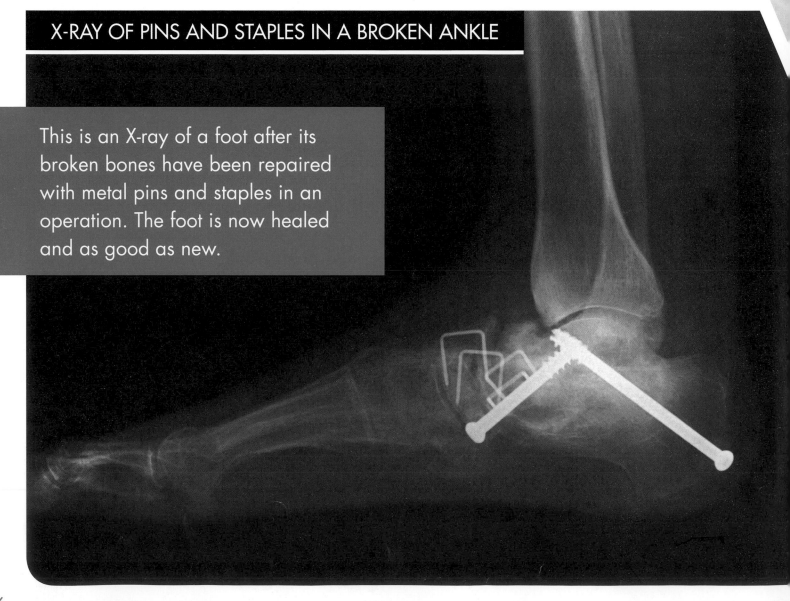

X-RAY OF PINS AND STAPLES IN A BROKEN ANKLE

This is an X-ray of a foot after its broken bones have been repaired with metal pins and staples in an operation. The foot is now healed and as good as new.

The one thing your bone needs to heal is rest. This means that you should not move it, even a tiny bit. That's why the bandage for a broken bone is a stiff cast that holds the break in a fixed position. Make friends with that cast. You're going to be wearing it for at least a month, possibly two.

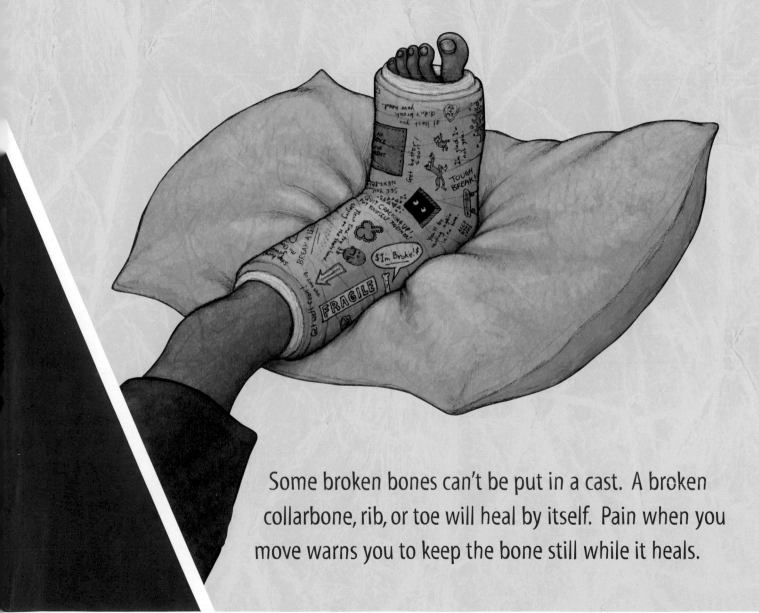

Some broken bones can't be put in a cast. A broken collarbone, rib, or toe will heal by itself. Pain when you move warns you to keep the bone still while it heals.

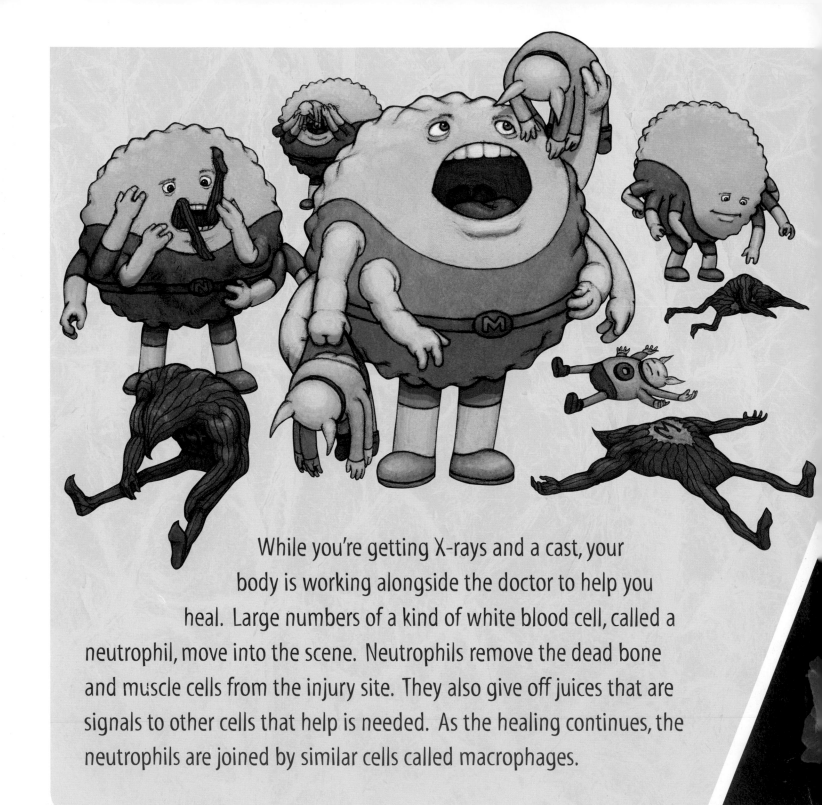

While you're getting X-rays and a cast, your
body is working alongside the doctor to help you
heal. Large numbers of a kind of white blood cell, called a
neutrophil, move into the scene. Neutrophils remove the dead bone
and muscle cells from the injury site. They also give off juices that are
signals to other cells that help is needed. As the healing continues, the
neutrophils are joined by similar cells called macrophages.

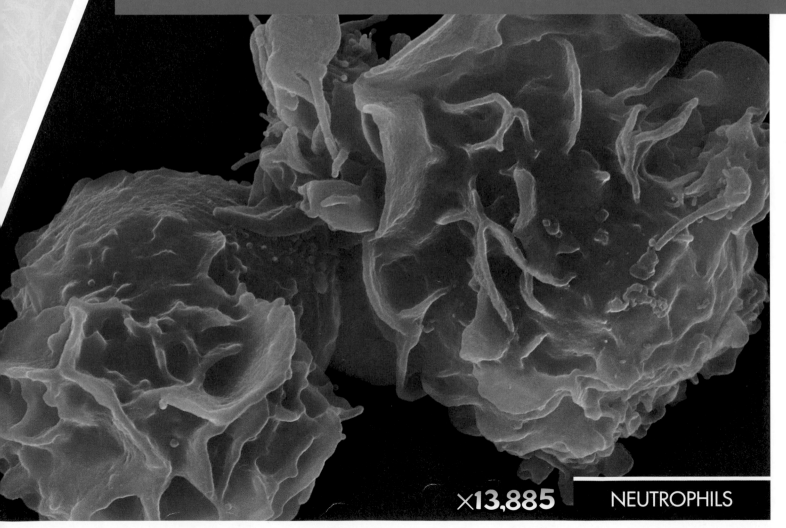

Neutrophils and similar cells called macrophages change shape by forming bulges on either side of a dead cell or germ. The bulges grow longer until they meet around the dead cell, which is then inside the neutrophil. Once inside, the neutrophil "digests" the dead cell. It continues this job until it, too dies. Later, macrophages come in to clean up any remainging debris on the battle site, including dead neutrophils.

×**13,885**   NEUTROPHILS

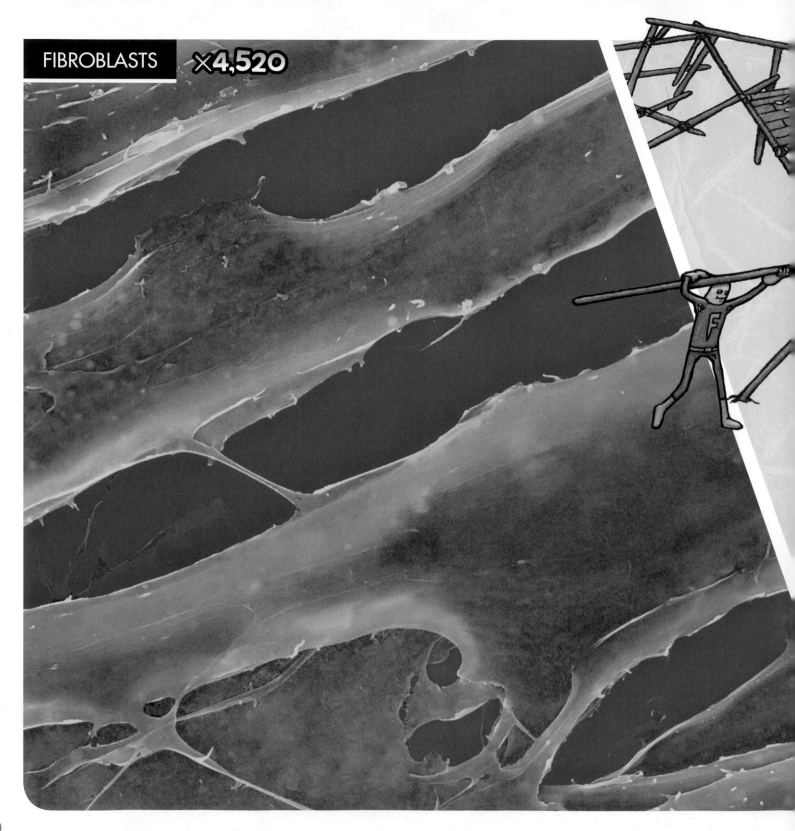

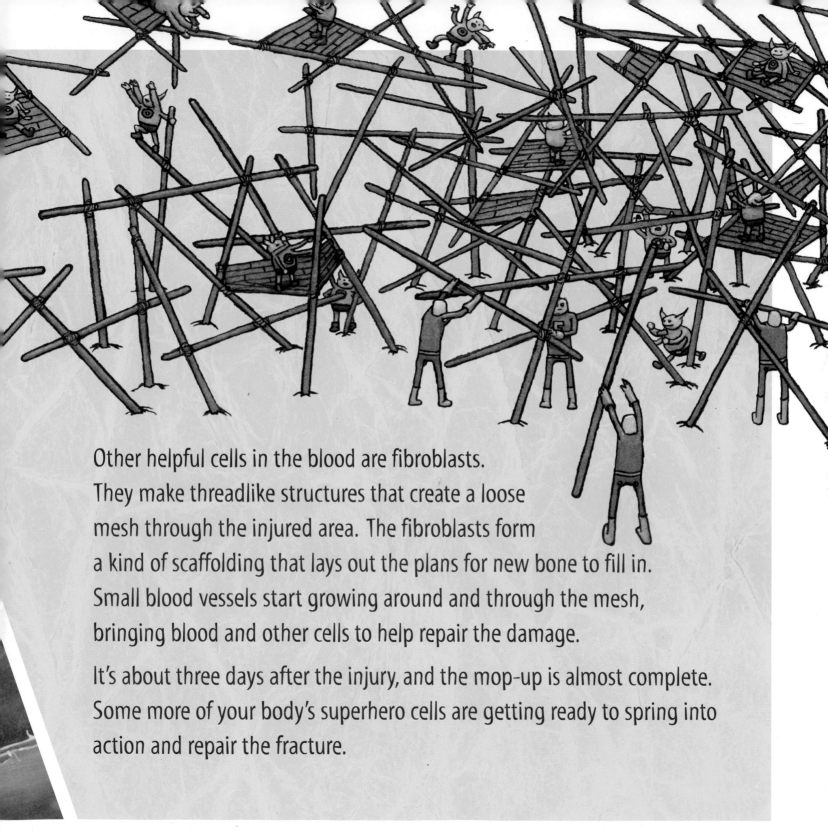

Other helpful cells in the blood are fibroblasts. They make threadlike structures that create a loose mesh through the injured area. The fibroblasts form a kind of scaffolding that lays out the plans for new bone to fill in. Small blood vessels start growing around and through the mesh, bringing blood and other cells to help repair the damage.

It's about three days after the injury, and the mop-up is almost complete. Some more of your body's superhero cells are getting ready to spring into action and repair the fracture.

Stem cells can become many other kinds of cells. They turn into the kinds of cells that build new bone at the break. Building new bone is complicated. Stem cells are the real heroes of the healing process.

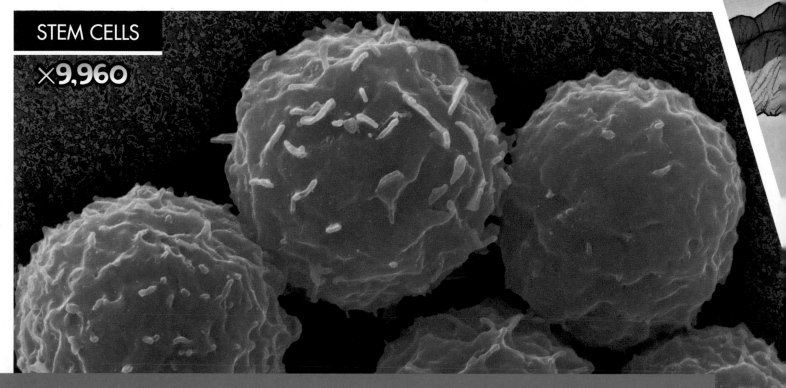

STEM CELLS

×9,960

Stem cells are truly amazing! Many scientists are doing research on them because of their ability to change into all kinds of different cells. Here's how. A stem cell splits into two parts. One part remains a stem cell, and the other becomes the new, needed cell. This new cell can reproduce others like itself. Healing a fracture is one natural way your body uses stem cells, but doctors and scientists are working on ways to use stem cells to cure other medical problems.

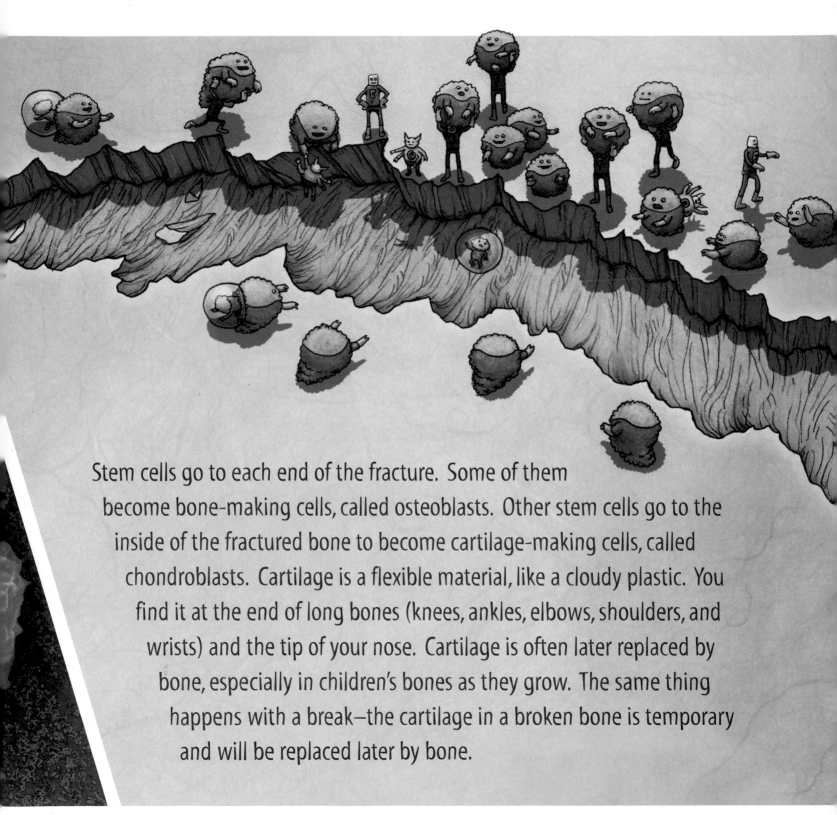

Stem cells go to each end of the fracture. Some of them become bone-making cells, called osteoblasts. Other stem cells go to the inside of the fractured bone to become cartilage-making cells, called chondroblasts. Cartilage is a flexible material, like a cloudy plastic. You find it at the end of long bones (knees, ankles, elbows, shoulders, and wrists) and the tip of your nose. Cartilage is often later replaced by bone, especially in children's bones as they grow. The same thing happens with a break—the cartilage in a broken bone is temporary and will be replaced later by bone.

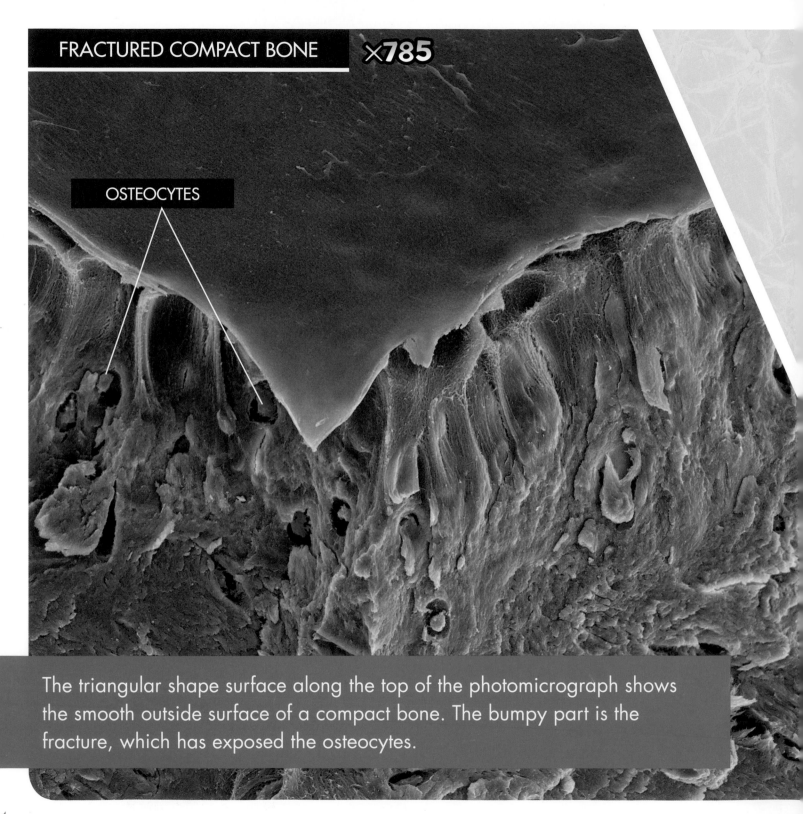

FRACTURED COMPACT BONE ×785

OSTEOCYTES

The triangular shape surface along the top of the photomicrograph shows the smooth outside surface of a compact bone. The bumpy part is the fracture, which has exposed the osteocytes.

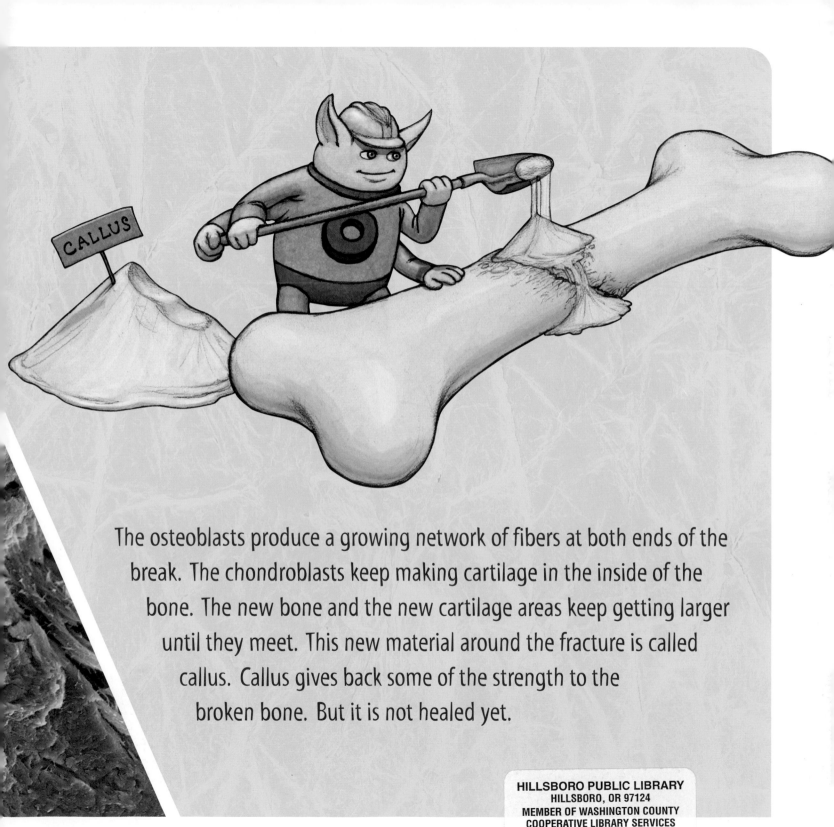

The osteoblasts produce a growing network of fibers at both ends of the break. The chondroblasts keep making cartilage in the inside of the bone. The new bone and the new cartilage areas keep getting larger until they meet. This new material around the fracture is called callus. Callus gives back some of the strength to the broken bone. But it is not healed yet.

Blood carries minerals to the woven bone and cartilage to make them stronger. About two weeks after the fracture, new cell workers, the osteoclasts, show up. The callus of woven bone and cartilage is disorganized compared to your original bone, which was formed in beautiful tiny layers.

So the osteoclasts dissolve the quickly made callus. The osteoblasts start laying down new bone. After a month or two, the fracture is strong enough that the cast can come off. And *still* the healing isn't finished.

The doctor will remove your cast with a saw. Your skin will be pale with a whitish coating on it. Your skin is always shedding dead skin cells, and normally they just fall off. But the cast prevents this from happening, so the coating of dead skin cells piles up. A good scrubbing in a bath or shower should solve the problem.

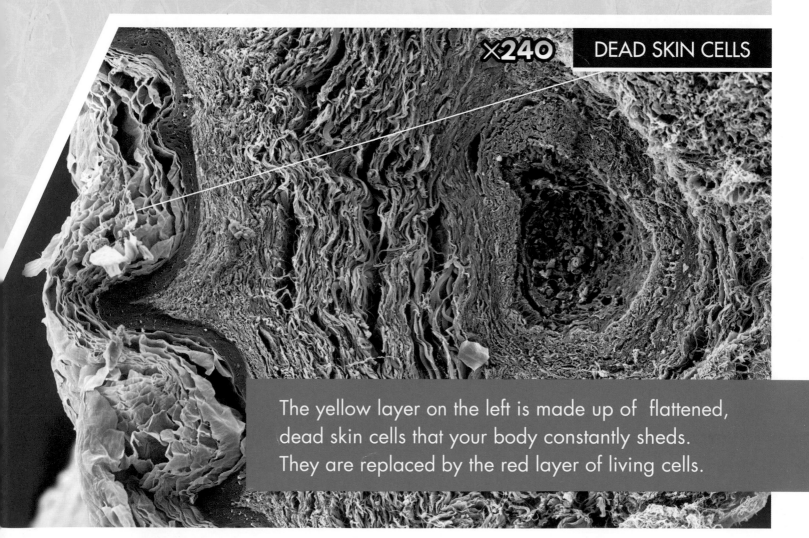

×240   DEAD SKIN CELLS

The yellow layer on the left is made up of flattened, dead skin cells that your body constantly sheds. They are replaced by the red layer of living cells.

Your arm or leg will also look skinnier than your unbroken limb. When you don't use your muscles, they shrink. Since you've been in a cast, you've lost some muscle. But a few weeks of using your muscles again will make them come back to normal.

The bone cells need to feel the pull and push of your muscles. Activity helps the bone cells to make sure the bone is just the right size and shape to support your muscles. Your body actually remembers the shape and design of your original bone.

About three months after a fracture, your healed bone is as good as new. Doctors have discovered that you must use your bones to keep them healthy. So celebrate your healed bone by running, skipping, and jumping. The more you exercise your bones, the stronger they become.

GLOSSARY

blood vessels: tubes that carry blood

bone marrow: the soft tissue found in the hollow insides of bones. Red blood cells are produced here.

calcium: an element that is absorbed by the body and makes bones hard

callus: a temporary structure of fibroblasts and chondroblasts that forms around a broken bone at the beginning of the healing process

cartilage: a flexible connective tissue that is found at the ends of long bones, in the nose, and in the outer ear

cells: the smallest units of all living things considered to be alive. The smallest living things have only one cell. Humans are multicelled.

chondroblasts: cells that make cartilage

compact bone: hard, dense bone that makes up most of the outside layers of bones of the body. It is packed with calcium.

fibroblasts: cells that form connective tissue fibers. They are especially important in repairing a wound.

fracture: a crack or break in a bone

macrophage: a white blood cell that cleans up sick and infected areas by "eating" germs and dead cells

minerals: compounds in nature with definite chemical formulas

osteoblasts: cells that make new bone cells

osteoclasts: cells that dissolve bone cells by reabsorbing the calcium. They are essential for reshaping a bone as it heals from a fracture.

osteocytes: star-shaped cells trapped deep inside compact bones that help maintain the minerals in compact bone. They are originally osteoblasts.

photomicrograph: a photograph taken with the help of a microscope

red blood cells: the cells in the blood that carry oxygen to all parts of the body. Their red color comes from iron in each cell.

spongy bone: a layer of honeycomb-like bone lining the hollow insides of long bones surrounding the marrow cavity

stem cells: immature cells that are capable of making many other types of cells

white blood cells: colorless cells floating in the blood that help the body fight disease

X-ray: a photograph that doctors use to see how a bone has been fractured

FURTHER READING

Arnold, Caroline. *The Skeletal System*. Minneapolis: Lerner Publications Company, 2005.

Ballard, Carol. *Bones*. Portsmouth, NH: Heinemann, 2002.

MacNair, Patricia Ann. *Movers & Shapers: Bones, Muscles, and Joints*. London: Kingfisher, 2004.

Silverstein, Alvin, Virginia Silverstein, and Laura Silverstein Nunn. *Broken Bones*. Danbury, CT: Franklin Watts, 2000.

Simon, Seymour. *Bones: Our Skeletal System*. New York: Harper Trophy, 2000.

WEBSITES

The Children's Hospital, Colorado
http://www.thechildrenshospital.org/wellness/info/parents/21755.aspx
Although designed for parents, the site gives a clear explanation of how to know if a bone is broken and what to do if it is. It also discusses different types of fractures and different kinds of casts.

Children's Museum of Indianapolis Bones: An Exhibit Inside You
http://www.childrensmuseum.org/special_exhibits/bones/kids_mazeGame.htm
A number of games that offer information about bones. The site also features an excellent group of links to other websites on bones.

KidsHealth
http://www.kidshealth.org/kid/exercise/safety/broken_bones.html
A site called *The Facts about Broken Bones* offers details on various kinds of bone fractures.

http://www.kidshealth.org/kid/body/bones_noSW.html
The Big Story on Bones is an extremely kid-friendly site on the structure of bones.

University of Washington
http://depts.washington.edu/bonebio/
Designed for middle school students, the *Bone Biology for Kids* site was created and is maintained by Dr. Susan Ott, who acted as a consultant on this book. It contains some excellent drawings and photographs of bone development.

INDEX

bold entries indicate photomicrographs

blood cell, 3, 29. *See also* red blood cells; white blood cells
blood vessel, **6**, **10**, 11, 12, **13**, 21
bone cell, 5, **6**, 29
bone marrow cavity, **6**, 10
bones, 4; kinds of, **6**, 9. *See also* compact bone; spongy bone
broken bone, 3, 12, 14, 23–25; healing, 17–26. *See also* fracture
calcium, 7
callus, 25–26
cartilage, 23, 25–26

cast, 17, 18, 26–27
cell, 3–5. *See also* blood cell; bone cell; dead cell; muscle cell; nerve cell; stem cell
chondroblasts, 23, 25
compact bone, 6–7, **10**, **23**
dead cell, 12, 18–19, **27**
fibroblasts, 3, **20**–21
fracture, 21, **22**–**24**, 29. *See also* broken bone
macrophage, 3, 18–**19**
microscope, 5, 6
muscle cell, **5**, 12, 18

muscles, 4, 28–29
nerve cell, **5**
neutrophils, 3, 18–**19**
osteoblasts, 3, 23, 25
osteoclasts, 26
osteocytes, 6–7, **11**, **24**
red blood cells, 5, 9, 11–12, **13**
red bone marrow, 8–9
spongy bone, **8**–9
stem cell, 3, 10, 11, **22**–23
white blood cells, 9, 11–12, 18
X–ray, **14**, 16, 18
yellow bone marrow, 10–11